Leading Ordinary Churches into Growth

Alan Howe

Area Dean of West Nottingham

GROVE BOOKS LIMITED
RIDLEY HALL RD CAMBRIDGE CB3 9HU

Contents

Church Army supports the Grove Evangelism Series

Church Army is a society of evangelists within the Anglican Communion that trains, supports and deploys evangelists across the UK and Ireland to enable people to come to a living faith in Jesus Christ.

Church Army—sharing faith through words and action

For more information about Church Army go to www.churcharmy.org.uk or phone 0208 309 3519 or email info@churcharmy.org.uk

Church Army, Marlowe House, 109 Station Rd, Sidcup, Kent DA15 7AD
Registered Charity number: 226226

The Cover Illustration is by Peter Ashton

First Impression May 2005
ISSN 1367-0840
ISBN 1 85174 592 0

Why This Booklet Was Written

1

> *'On five occasions in history the church has gone to the dogs,
> but on each occasion it was the dogs that died.'*
>
> *G K Chesterton*[1]

I believe that continued decline in congregational numbers in the ordinary churches is not inevitable. Church history has known both ebbs and flows. In what follows, I have sought to illustrate that growth can happen even when struggling against the tide.

This study forms part of a search for leadership insights and tools that will help make that turnaround possible in the church where I lead, and in other ordinary churches across the country. It could be used alongside a previous booklet in the Evangelism series, *How to Develop a Mission Strategy* by Jim Currin.[2] Both booklets contain material that can be photocopied and used with a leadership team.

This work is in an Anglican context. It draws on examples from Anglican churches in order to give a meaningful research sample and because access to data for these churches was readily available. It is, however, written in an ecumenical spirit and I believe the insights gained to be transferable to the settings of leaders in partner churches. I have sought to explain Anglican terms as they arise.

Transforming Leadership?

David Bosch's seminal work *Transforming Mission*[3] introduces the concept of the development of Christian mission not happening as a steady process but rather in a series of more acute 'paradigm shifts.' I am convinced by his argument, but would go further and postulate that the same is true in microcosm with an individual leader's approach to the mission task. Having begun to think along those lines it was encouraging to find others already thinking in this direction. Brian Pettifer, writing in the excellent and stimulating collection of studies for the (MODEM)[4] publication *Management and Ministry*,[5] argues that the leadership context for ministry in the 21st century is so different from previous realities that a paradigm shift is required in the way leaders think and act.

The moderately growing churches in Greater Nottingham selected for study provided the context for me to engage in the analysis of how one group of leaders are making such a shift. I have listened to their stories and noted the tools they used to help their churches grow. Some used a primarily strategic approach; others majored on building relational strength; all of them took time to listen to their fellow leaders and to their context. All of them sought to have ears that heard what the Spirit was saying to the church. There were no 'one size fits all' answers but their hope and my hope is that there is something in what follows that will help you.

The Wider Context?

The Christian church has been growing for 2,000 years. From a group of 12 disciples it has grown to a world-wide fellowship of 2 billion people. Globally, there is still no evidence of decline and the most recent research shows the rate of growth of the church matching the exponential population explosion. More than half the Christians that have ever lived are still alive! However, this heady story of growth has not been the recent experience of the Western world and definitely not in the experience of the European West, where the story since the end of the First World War has been one of constant decline.

	1950 membership	1970 membership	1990 membership
Protestant	6.1	5.2	3.4
All Christian	9.6	7.9	5.6

Table 1: Christian church membership in Britain (millions) 1950–1990

These figures, researched by the sociologist Steve Bruce,[6] only tell part of the story because membership is not the same as actual attendance. That figure is much lower; Peter Brierley gives figures for 1998 that show a total attendance for Protestant churches of 1.4 million and all Christian churches of 2.4 million.[7] A typically 'modern' approach to addressing this disturbing decline has been the application of some scientific method. It was Donald McGavran, writing in 1970, who declared that church growth is a process which 'is extremely complex and which must be understood with care.'[8] Not only that, but McGavran also asserts that failure to grow could be viewed as a disease which is curable.

Is such a cure possible in 2005? This research on leading ordinary local churches into growth starts from the premise that churches which are growing can provide insights that can help those who seek to lead churches that are static or in decline to make the transition into a more positive state of growth.

This booklet looks at seven churches in the Nottingham area which grew by 20% or more in the period 1998 to 2002. Are there leadership insights that are transferable to other churches?

Some factors will be the result of unique phenomena in the make-up of the locality or the mix of leadership gifts within those churches. It is also likely that some good practice can, with care, be adopted and applied to similar parishes in the wider church.

Why Study This Topic Now?

The Bad News

The church has been addressing the challenge faced by the decline of Christianity in the West for at least 35 years. Whilst some individual churches and some denominations have seen growth during this period, all the research, until recently, has been pointing to an overall picture of continued decline. Peter Brierley cuts to the quick with the title of his excellent but disturbing statistical analysis, *The Tide is Running Out*. Amongst a host of sobering facts, one of the starkest is that 12% of the population of the people in England attended church in 1979 compared with only 7.5% in 1998, a staggering 38% decline.[9] As my study is centred on Anglican churches, the clear and well-presented 2002 study by Bob Jackson adds to the picture painted by Brierley with some specific denominational statistics. Figures for the Southwell diocese for the period 1989-1999 show a decline in usual Sunday attendance by adults of 16% and of children by a heartbreaking 34%.[10]

The Good News

One factor as to why 'now' presents a good time for a study is that the urgency of the task which faces the whole western church has produced a crop of excellent and relevant literature which seeks to help the local church leader looking to promote growth. Two books which have proved particularly helpful are recent publications from Church House Publishing: The Church of England Mission and Public Affairs working party report, *Mission-Shaped Church: Church Planting and Fresh Expressions of Church in a Changing Context*[11] and the excellent summary of contemporary strategies for evangelism by Booker and Ireland, *Evangelism: Which Way Now?*[12] Another key resource has been a book by Robert Warren, *The Healthy Churches Handbook*[13] which resonates with some of the insights of Christian Schwarz's, *Natural Church Development*[14] thinking. I found Warren's approach simpler and more earthed for parish use. Warren includes analytical exercises, one of which has been employed in this study within the focus group setting as described later. Focus group members warmed to the vision of 'healthy church' and took on the study with enthusiasm.

Why Choose Greater Nottingham as the Area of Study?

The motivation for this research came initially from a chance discussion between a group of Area Deans[15] within the Nottingham Archdeaconry.[16] The group of eight incumbents were sharing positive stories over a working breakfast. One incumbent was thrilled by the exciting growth in his congregation and the story told encouraged all present. His account was brought to a close with a throwaway comment. 'No one will ever write a book about our story but it has been a joy to be part of it!' As Area Dean of West Nottingham, I was one of those present, and reflected long and hard on that comment. Books tend to be written about the leadership of 'mega churches' or churches that abound in trendy signs, wonders and manifestations of one kind or another. Such churches and their leaders can be admired but they are hard to emulate. However, at any given point in time a huge number of churches are experiencing moderate growth. Later results will show that 108 of 283 parishes in the diocese were exhibiting some growth (identical percentages [38%] for each of the two Archdeaconries) and 27 of those churches were growing by

Books tend to be written about the leadership of 'mega churches'

20% or more in the research period 1998–2002. The Southwell diocese and the Greater Nottingham area boast no mega churches. No single Anglican church in the diocese has a usual Sunday attendance of more than 350. If there are growth stories worth telling then those stories will come from those 27 churches exhibiting moderate growth. This study explores the stories of seven out of the 17 moderately growing churches from the Nottingham Archdeaconry.

The Tide Flows in Both Directions

To pick up Brierley's tidal analogy, it is the nature of tides to both ebb and flow. The research conducted for this booklet recorded usual Sunday attendances for every parish in the Anglican Diocese of Southwell over the five year period 1998 to 2002 in order to determine the best sample of churches to study in depth. This research produced somewhat surprising results. I plotted a simple graph for all the parishes in the diocese. The graph shown as figure 1 gives a plot to left of centre for every church which experienced decline over the period and to the right of centre for every church that experienced growth. The growth and decline axis shows decline or growth in terms of numbers of people. The range was wide with one church adding 62 and another losing 61! All 283 churches are represented but blend to give the overall shape. Conditioned as described above to expect a shape that expressed decline, the actual shape of the graph came as a surprise. This surprise struck me as good news and it will be good news to every church leader reading this booklet.

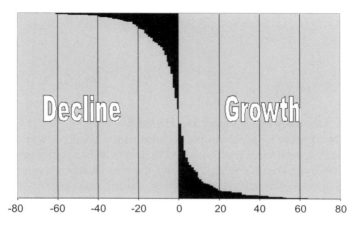

Figure 1: Numerical Change in all 259
Parishes in the Southwell Diocese 1998–2002

The statistics actually express a mere 1% decline over 5 years across the diocese. This tiny percentage decline is lost in the overall impression which is that both sides of the graph appear the same. This means that in the Diocese of Southwell decline is far from inevitable. Put at its simplest, the message of these findings is that:

> The difference between 'growth' and 'decline' in the average Anglican church is to be doing a little better than average.
>
> Based on figures for the Diocese of Southwell

Weary leaders with years of experience at the coal face may have picked up this study with the expectation that the transition from decline to growth in the inherited expression of church they have been called to lead is going to involve some huge project or fundamental change. I have plenty of sympathy with such expectations, having dredged books and tapes for such insights for decades! The truth from these statistics is somewhat different. Change and new projects may indeed be required, but the transition from 5% decline to 5% increase may not be the kind of huge leap that will grind them into exhaustion. Further figures becoming available for 2003 show a small positive development in attendance trends, moving the chart to a point of parity.[17] Total attendance in Southwell in 2002 was 19,800 and in 2003 that figure had risen slightly to 19,900.

2

The Seven Churches

St Mary's, Attenborough—Vicar: Sue Hemsley
St Mary's is a parish of 4,500 people 5 miles to the west of Nottingham. The church building is picturesquely situated in the midst of a nature reserve on the banks of the River Trent. The area around the church has a strong traditional village feel; a cricket match was in progress during one research visit! Demographically, the church is cut off by a railway line from most of the parish and although there is a dense modern housing development in the north of the parish it is further isolated by an 'A' road aptly named By Pass Road. The primary challenge facing the leaders was to cross some physical and some sociological barriers and make the church more friendly and inclusive. In 1998 the returns showed a usual Sunday attendance of 85 adults. Growth was a little erratic but by 2002 the figure had increased by an encouraging 36% to 116.

Holy Trinity, Clifton—Vicar until 2004: Eric Forshaw
Holy Trinity forms one part of a three-church Team Ministry in Clifton, a post-war council/owner occupier estate on the south bank of the River Trent. The team ministers to just fewer than 20,000 people, of whom around 4,000 fall under the pastoral care of Holy Trinity. There is an urban feel to the estate but no great evidence of vandalism and the houses are mostly well kept and cared for. There are two pockets of high deprivation. An additional challenge facing leaders was planning for growth in an area with a very high proportion of elderly people. Holy Trinity is well located opposite a bustling parade of shops and is physically highly visible within the estate. The church building is modern and functional in design but has some interesting architectural touches. Growth at Holy Trinity has been slow but gloriously consistent over the research sample period. The 1998 returns showed a usual adult Sunday attendance of 44 rising in increments of two to three a year to 55 in 2002, a growth of 23.5%. All the indications are that this steady growth is continuing in spite of the church currently being in interregnum, which provides evidence that lay leaders have been well trained and envisioned.

St Paul's, Daybrook—Vicar: Chris Rattenberry
The area of Daybrook forms part of North Nottingham and straddles a main 'A' road. It is a varied area containing a cross section of housing and a major urban estate which is an area of some deprivation. It is a numerically large multi-ethnic parish of just under 10,000 people. The parish has two worship

centres. The main parish church of St Paul is a splendid example of late Victoriana (it is hard to miss in its dominant position on the main road). The mission church of St Timothy's is on the estate. The primary challenge facing the current leaders was to build stability with the arrival of the third ordained leader in a short period. With 85 worshippers in 1998 and 139 in 2002 (many more were present when I visited in 2004 and the congregation reflected the ethnic balance of the community), it is the church that showed the highest numerical growth in the Diocese of Southwell for the given research period.

St Luke's, Gamston—Vicar: Steve Silvester
The parish of St Luke's, Gamston is situated to the south of the River Trent on the eastern fringe of West Bridgford. The church building is modern and recently refurbished and greatly extended. It is an excellent multifunctional plant, with a building which though light and open manages to retain an air of spiritual focus. The first impression is of a post-war estate without a great deal of character. The housing varies greatly and there is no sense of depravation or any particular evidence of vandalism. To this estate has been added a much more modern development of housing suited to young professionals and young families with children, which has doubled the size of the parish to 7,462. The new estate fits geographically snugly into the parish catchment and is bounded by the main two main roads. A challenge that faced the leadership was how to best change church structures to meet the needs of a rapidly growing area. Numbers have risen from 90 in 1998 to 121 in 2002 and growth has continued at an increased pace following the addition of an extra service. There is a large and able lay leadership team.

St James, Papplewick and St Michael's, Linby—Vicar: Keith Turner
Papplewick is 8 miles north of Nottingham and 1 mile east of Hucknall and boasts a population of 620 in 250 dwellings. It is a pretty village with a strong sense of community and incorporates a school, a pub and a village hall. It has a place in history marking the southern gate to Sherwood Forest. The area covered by the parish of Linby takes in part of Hucknall and has a larger population touching on 5,000. There is a real sense of the rural about these two villages as evidenced by the fact that I was delayed in my attempt to attend the service at Papplewick by a herd of cows that blocked the road! The two parishes work well together and both are used to provide a varied pattern of worship with four services a month at Papplewick and six at Linby. The church building of St Michael's is more accessible and it is there that the best attended service of the month takes place (the Family Service). Both buildings are assets and have a strong sense of history and spirituality.

There is an exciting development project in the offing to reorder the church building at Linby to make it more flexible and adaptable to currents needs and usage, without losing the valuable sense of tradition. The churches showed encouraging steady growth during the period 1998–2002 with average Sunday attendance climbing from 62 to 79. The ongoing challenge for the leadership team is to preserve the hard won sense of unity at the same time as promoting the change required for growth.

St Patrick's, Nuthall—Vicar: Janet Henderson

Nuthall (population 6,206) is a popular residential area much favoured by commuters to Nottingham and close to Junction 26 of the M1. Much of the population of the parish live on two estates separated from the historic village by main roads. One of these estates is recent and typical of many that have sprung up all around Nottingham in the past 10–15 years. St Patrick's holds monthly services on this estate. The church building oozes history and spirituality but it is amazingly small and scarcely able to house its growing congregation. This problem of physical space is very real for the congregation at this point and figured prominently in the focus group discussion. Handling this issue is probably the next big challenge for the leadership team. The church has a good sized hall close by and this is used for the occasional acts of worship termed 'community services.' There are three services on the average Sunday at 8.45, 10.30 and 6.30. All three are acknowledged as important and it is recognized that they appeal to different sections of the worshipping community. The 10.30 service is the one that has seen the most growth, from a low point of 19 attendees five years ago to a congregation of around 70 at the research visit in July 2004. Overall the attendance grew from 60 in 1998 to 91 in 2002 and growth continues.

St Wilfrid's, Wilford—Vicar: David Rowe

The parish is situated on the south bank of the River Trent about two miles west of Trent Bridge. It is a historic parish and parts of the church date back to the 13th century. The church is classically picturesque and the immediate surrounding area retains a strong village feel. The wider parish numbers 7,054 people and falls into three fairly distinct demographic areas. To the west of the main 'A' road lies an upwardly mobile estate of less expensive housing that retains some council houses but is now mostly owner occupied. Some of the residents have moved out of a nearby less prestigious estate and are pleased to identify themselves with Wilford. In spite of the apparent geographical remoteness of the church building a good number of people from this estate attend worship. There is a monthly service at the community centre and the possibility of a church plant has been explored and remains a possible option for the future. To the east of the main road lies a more modern 'up market' estate with many young professionals. The population divides approximately equally between the three areas. Wilford village retains its focal place for all three areas and this focus is cemented by the existence of a large secondary school and a church primary school. The leadership team have set themselves the challenge of integrating its large number of children and young people into the worship and service of the church. Numbers have gone from 70 in 1998 to 97 in 2002 and continue to increase. Well over 100 were at the service I attended in 2004.

How and Why These Seven Churches Were Chosen

The nature of the research method meant that the seven churches were largely self selecting. The numerical criteria produced 27 churches growing by 20% or more during the selected time frame. The decision to apply a geographical element to the selection (the Greater Nottingham Area) then produced the seven parishes. As can be seen from the descriptions, within the limitation of such a small sample quite a good mix of church style, type of area and sociological profile was achieved. There where no churches at the theological extremes and no city centre churches because no churches in these categories met the research criteria. Information was gathered using a mix of research tools.

1 I visited each church during a normal Sunday Service to see leadership in action and gathered similar data for each church.

2 I conducted a two-hour informal interview with the incumbent of each church during which we worked through a check list of questions. There was plenty of flexibility as we sought together to isolate the factors that had promoted growth in the churches they led.

3 In each church I held a 'focus group,' drawing together 7–10 lay leaders and church members not including the incumbent or other ordained leaders. Again the format was relaxed and I encouraged members to share their understanding of the growth process.

The following chapter draws some of the results of the research together. It seeks to avoid too many detailed specifics from each parish, preferring to look at general principles. This avoids embarrassment and maintains confidentiality. It also allowed me to step outside specific situations that may be locally relevant but not so easy for readers to apply to their own settings. In all seven focus groups members expressed their appreciation of the part played by their incumbent as leader of the team in working with them to provide a vision and a strategy for growth. At no stage over seven meetings with a total of 60 church members did any of them express a negative comment about the vicar or other ordained leaders. This seems to show, within the limitation of the research sample, that a connection exists between good relationships in the leadership team and numerical growth. The following chapter explores other leadership qualities that emerged from my research.

3 Leadership Qualities Equated with Leaders of Growing Churches

1 Leaders of Growing Churches have the Spiritual Gift of Leadership

> We have different gifts, according to the grace given us. If a person's gift is leadership, let them govern diligently (Romans 12.6–8).

> Christian leaders are unique in having a strong sense of who they are as God's servants. What is unique about them beyond this? The answer is nothing.[18]

> Knowing that we are chosen is at the heart of leadership.[19]

It is no surprise that this first finding from the research should be that the seven leaders interviewed displayed ample evidence of being effective leaders, displaying qualities that accompany the leadership gift. This booklet offers no magic insights for clerical or lay leaders who are looking for short cuts to growth, separate from the inspiration and the perspiration of the day to day leadership task. This group of leaders displayed evidence of leadership that goes beyond the local parish setting. Without exception they were all involved in additional work outside the parish as well as the long hours within it. This frees them from becoming 'parochial' (in the pejorative sense) and enables them to discover insights from other settings to apply in the local situation. Two were Area Deans, one was a member of Bishop's Council, another the Dean of Women's ministry and several acted in a variety of chaplaincy roles. They were all aware of the importance of leadership and all saw the need for constant formation of their leadership skills.

What If I am a Leader But Do Not Feel I Have These Gifts?

(This includes me on a bad day!) The description above could be discouraging for those readers who feel their leadership gifting to be very limited and, as declared earlier, this booklet aims to encourage rather than daunt. Of course every significant leader feels their gift to be limited ('I am the least of the apostles'—St Paul). If you are an ordained leader you will be an individual in whom the wider church has discerned both gifting and calling. You may not consider yourself very gifted, but others do. If you exercise any leadership role within the local church then you also have had that gifting recognized in some form. You did not just wake up one morning and decide to be a leader. You were in some way encouraged and trained by others within your congregation who discerned in you a measure of the leadership gift. For ordained and lay leaders, the fact that you have taken time and energy to select and read this booklet shows you are motivated to action that will improve your leadership skills and that you are interested in any insight that the leaders of seven moderately growing churches may have for you. You are already on the road to doing better than average and therefore ready to take advantage of the turning tide.

Case Study 1

A member of one of the seven focus groups spoke of their vicar's arrival. 'We had been through a number of vicars in quite a short time. It was with no great excitement or expectation I went to the first PCC meeting conducted by the new vicar. When he came in dragging a flip chart and pens I thought "Oh no! What's all this about?" He sensed our dismay and said, "Don't worry about this—it is my comfort blanket!" We laughed and continued to laugh as he painted a picture of his hopes for his time with us. It was like a light going on inside me. I said to myself "I think this one is going to crack it."'

That vicar, Chris Rattenberry, has led St Paul's, Daybrook in several years of successful moderate growth. Chris's sense of humour, gentle style and flexibility continue to maintain the relational health for ongoing growth.

Case Study 2

Does the theory work in practice? This was the question that drew Canon Janet Henderson away from her work as a theological college tutor and into parish work at St Patrick's, Nuthall in 2001. On paper St Patrick's seemed to have a lot of potential, with three services per Sunday each with a small but viable congregation and making a usual combined Sunday attendance of 60. However, at the start of her time there came a cold Sunday morning at the main 10.30 service when even in the tiny worship area her voice seemed to echo and she counted 19 people. Had she made the right step? She knew the theory and her strategic tool of choice was the Natural Church Development insights of Christian Schwartz. The theory which looks so colourful and elegant in all the manuals; could it work here in the ex-mining suburbs of Nottingham, in this tradition-soaked church with its semi-feudal history? This is where a leader needs to lead. In a traditional area Janet majored on traditional ministry. She got to work, forging closer links with schools, and if process evangelism were needed why not start with some confirmation courses? The latter proved outstandingly popular, and before long 40 people had been confirmed, 28 of them adults. By 2002 a Parish Plan was in place, approved by the PCC. After just three years usual Sunday attendance was up by 50%, with 92 people in church. At the parish visit in 2004 the problem for me as visitor was not the empty echo but rather finding a seat at all! The focus group was a delightful and positive group, quick to acknowledge Janet's leadership as the engine for growth. One summed it up. When I asked her why she thought the church was growing she replied 'We have a hard working vicar who works within the community, encouraging people to worship God.' Janet herself sees it more in terms of a team effort. When I asked her about reasons for the encouraging growth, she made reference to the support and hard work of her church members.

2 They Are Able to Think and Act Strategically and to Promote Strategic Action in Others

A 2003 representative survey of 1,125 churches conducted by Christian Research showed that only 25% of those churches had a long term strategic plan.[20]

Interestingly, the concept of the leader as a strategist gets precious little mention in two recent specific excellent writings on Christian leadership. The Bill Hybels magnum opus *Courageous Leadership*[21] and *Growing Leaders*[22] by James Lawrence concentrate quite rightly on the values that underpin the life of the leader and the ability of a leader to discern and communicate vision. Both books, however, give little space to the basic aspects of strategic thinking. The closest Lawrence gets is to talk of the need to identify 'process' and listen to 'context' but this is a sparse four pages in a 300-page book.[23] The quality I noted in discussion with the incumbents resonates more closely with the 'church growth' language of 20 years ago. Roy Pointer devotes a major section of *How Do Churches Grow*[24] to the two practical exercises of

a   Getting Organized for Growth
b   Planning for Growth

Some Anglican dioceses have given strong encouragement for their parishes to take a common approach to strategic thinking. They have either used in-house material or drawn on material produced by resource organizations such as Springboard, and recently the *Healthy Church Handbook*[25] by Canon Robert Warren has proved popular. This takes a Natural Church Development style approach by using an exercise based on measuring the health of a church in seven key areas. It then encourages a strategy that works first on the area deemed least healthy. I also commend a previous booklet in this series, *How to Develop a Mission Strategy* by Jim Currin, which is full of clear, practical and easy-to-use tools and exercises.[26]

In fact there is no shortage of tools available to the leader wishing to think strategically. During the five year period in which statistics were gathered, the Diocese of Southwell had two separate tools available from in-house advisors, both in their different ways building on the techniques of mission audit. Many parishes made use of one or other tool and still others discovered or devised their own tools. Using tools to gather information is only ever part of the story. Having a wonderful tool kit does not make a skilled carpenter. All the leaders in the sample group used tools to gather strategic information. What is more significant is that they knew how to turn information into action. Robert Warren gets to the root of the vital next stage with his summary of the implementation process.[27] This follows the isolation of the general course of action and it is where clear leadership is most needed in identifying:

- what is going to be done
- by whom
- with what resources
- in what timescale
- accountable to whom
- monitored by whom

It is hard to overstate the importance of this step in taking good research and turning it into action. The two case studies which follow are examples of good practice.

Case Study 3

Canon Eric Forshaw was Team Rector of Clifton, an 'out of town' estate containing a mix of council and owner-occupied housing. Eric was responsible for the team of several churches, but lived near and was himself based at Holy Trinity. The church building is set amid an ageing section of the community and Eric quickly discerned the need for some strategic thinking. From his own wide range of experience he decided to use a secular tool called 'Investors in People,' and in addition he called on the aid of a diocesan mission audit advisor. Eric needed to decide how to motivate a group of people that contained few natural leaders, and hit on a two-stage strategy that has proved very effective. Using a 'process' nurture and evangelism course, *Emmaus*, he established six small groups. Relationships were formed in these groups and the same groups, once established, became the groups that carried out the spade work of mission audit. As a result of the audit process it was realized that the area of ministry to invest most heavily in was pastoral care, especially the pastoral care of the recently bereaved. As a result of this gentle faithful ministry there has been a slow, steady increase in attendance but the gentle growth has proved sustainable.

Case Study 4

The Revd Sue Hemsley came to the pretty Trent-side church of St Mary's, Attenborough in 1999. The church had for some time lived in the shadow of its daughter church on the nearby Toton estate which as a lively and informal church in an area of numerical expansion had undergone healthy growth over an extended period.

St Mary's retained its village identity, and according to focus group members had become too rigid and formal, even gaining a reputation for being unfriendly in some quarters. After a period of settling in and establishing trust, Sue led the PCC in strategic thinking. They devoted a number of PCC meetings to developing a five-year plan. As the PCC worked at planning and began to see a future emerge, other changes began to happen. Relationships within the council became more positive and (according to focus group members) meetings changed from being hard work to becoming a joy that members looked forward to. The actual tools were not rocket science and began with a SWOT (strength and weakness, opportunity and threat) analysis. The resulting 5-year plan was strongly relational, with emphasis on building relationships in the village and making use of classical evangelistic opportunities. I had the opportunity to attend a stunning flower festival based on the C S Lewis' book *The Lion, the Witch and the Wardrobe*, which attracted large numbers of potential new contacts. A booklet was available explaining Christian truth from Lewis' book. Many visitors stayed to chat over coffee and the whole event was an example of good practice in contextual outreach.

3 They Are Able to Think and Act Relationally and to Promote Good Relationships Within the Churches that They Lead

Leadership is a relationship — a relationship in which one person seeks to influence the thoughts, behaviours and beliefs or values of another person. Transforming leadership is a relationship that raises the values and aspirations of both the leader and the follower to new levels.[28]

When asked what is the most important factor for church growth a staggering 81% of the 1,125 churches that took part in the Christian Research survey replied 'the warm welcome received.'[29]

One of the exercises carried out with the focus group in each church was the seven-point health check from Robert Warren's *Healthy Churches Handbook*. The results, shown as figure 2, proved significant.

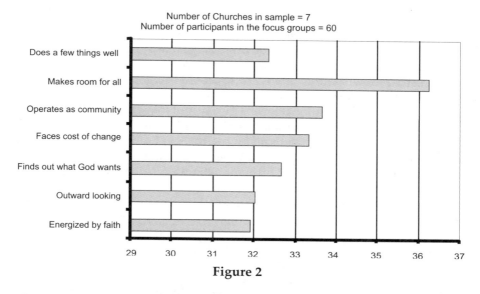

Number of Churches in sample = 7
Number of participants in the focus groups = 60

Does a few things well	
Makes room for all	
Operates as community	
Faces cost of change	
Finds out what God wants	
Outward looking	
Energized by faith	

29   30   31   32   33   34   35   36   37

Figure 2

The seven categories from the handbook are self explanatory; the numbers need some explanation. Each of the seven churches gave itself a mark out of six in each category, averaging the scores of the individuals in the focus group. If everyone had thought their church was in perfect health, the maximum score would be six (points) times seven (churches) which is 42. So we can see that overall the churches felt themselves to be weakest in the category of 'energized by faith,' scoring 31.9 out of 42 (which is far from a bad score). But they were strongest in the two indicators of relational health, with 'making room for all' scoring three clear marks stronger than any other, at 36.3 out of 42.

From the three sources used in my research it was clear that this emphasis on the importance of relationships and in particular 'the welcome' came straight from the leadership of the seven churches. In a number of the churches it was acknowledged by the incumbent, reiterated in the focus group and picked up in conversation with congregational members that most of those churches had been through times when relationships were not going well. The nature of the various relationship breakdowns varied and all were of types frequently encountered in struggling churches. Without exception those leaders interviewed saw it as their job to model positive relationships. This was intentional and given high priority. A relational Christian leader is not simply concerned that a job is done but also with the relationship quality that accompanies the action. Wright brings some helpful insights: 'The fruit of the Spirit should be manifest in the work we do together...I believe strongly that we are to be leaders who reflect the presence of Christ in our communities.'[30]

Case Study 5
David Rowe returned to parish ministry after a period of joint leadership of a 'Willow Creek' style fresh expression of church, a role he combined with being one of the diocesan mission advisors. Members of the congregation at Wilford were keen to see what innovations David would bring. However, for several focus group members it was not new ideas they needed most. It was some positive input on the relational level. One faithful longer term member said: 'Things had been hard going for a long time. All my life I attended regularly but had hit a phase where the more I went, the less I seemed to get out of it. It became easier not to go than to go. When David arrived it only took a few services to rekindle the fire. He brought what we needed: enthusiasm, connectedness with the community and inspirational leadership.' Within a year the church also had a 26-page strategic plan, a plan permeated throughout with strategies that are strongly relational:

- Make church welcoming and user friendly
- Run events that encourage quality relationships
- Improve communication throughout the church family
- Build friendships in which we can tell our faith story
- Encourage wider participation using the whole variety of our gifts and talents.

It is easy for these things to be words on paper, but the Sunday visit showed that by 2004 they had become the values of the church. I was greeted three times, once outside the church by a sidesperson, conducted to my seat by a (polite!) teenager and instantly befriended by an older couple. David's leadership style embodies hospitality and it spreads like a wave throughout the church. Many churches have holiday clubs in the summer to contact local schools, but not many invite every child's family to a free feast that led to the feeding of over 1,000 people. The mission spin-off of this event was vast. One focus group member, the husband of a church member, said 'I had never been to church but was encouraged to become a helper at this meal and that started me on the road to personal faith.'

4 They Are Able to Think and Act Transformationally and to Promote Positive Change Within the Churches that They Lead

Vision is not just abstract idealism but practical reality in renewing your energy and seeking to turn decline into growth.

Peter Brierley[31]

This section moves into the area of vision, or rather what results from a positive response to an appropriately cast vision: transformation. Brierley, in an excellent article, introduces five telling questions taken directly from the Old Testament, each asked by God. He challenges his readers (those seeking to manage and minister) to use these questions in establishing a vision for the setting in which they have been chosen to lead. Any strategic approach drawn from such a source is bound to be pretty potent.

1 Where are you?—(God to Adam; Genesis 3.9) Hiding in the garden or ready to face the hard truth with God's help?

2 What is in your hand?—(God to Moses; Exodus 4.2) Just a staff? Our limited resources become special when used as God directs.

3 What are you doing here?—(God to Elijah; 1 Kings 19.9) Are you here by accident or by mistake or did God choose you for this?

4 What do you see?—(God to Jeremiah and Amos; Jeremiah 24.3, Amos 7.8) Through the eyes of faith—I see four new families with us this time next year!

5 Can these bones live?—(God to Ezekiel; Ezekiel 37.3) You know, Lord! If you give the word—yes they can.[32]

The booklet *Developing Visionary Leadership*,[33] by Richard Williams and Mark Tanner in the Grove Renewal series, also offers real practical insights in this area of turning vision into action that leads to change and growth in the local church.

The seven churches in the study were all ordinary. They had nothing special going for them. Several of them had been going through lean times, some looked back on a wake of hurt and discouragement, of depressed former leaders and discouraged current members. In all the settings some measure of transformation was needed.

Case Study 6
In 1996 Steve Silvester moved from leading an exciting church plant congregation to taking on the role of vicar at St Luke's, Gamston. With only 45 years of history from a beginning as a church of three wooden huts, St Luke's had developed and grown as a daughter church in the shadow of a bustling and prestigious parent church but was very much in need of a clear direction of its own to transform a faithful but tired congregation to one with a sense of excitement for the mission task. A new church building had been added, and another phase in the development of the plant was needed, but what exactly was the building to be for? Would it provide a resource for mission?

It was a new Christian, a local businessman, who challenged Steve with the straight question, 'What is your vision for St Luke's?' Here it is in Steve's own words:

> As I have prayed and shared and listened with other leaders in the church, the image that keeps returning is of the life-giving river described in Ezekiel chapter 47. The river flows from the temple, the place where God is worshipped. However, the further it flows from the temple, the deeper it becomes. My vision is for the life of God to flow from St Luke's in the same way!

The three words *come, receive, overflow* came to form the ethos of a genuinely vibrant church. It is no longer just Steve's vision, for it is shared by the rapidly expanding congregation. I have visited the church on three occasions and each time it has been healthily crammed. It was necessary to add an extra congregation to cope with the influx. Evidence that the vision has been caught comes from the focus group responses. 'St Luke's is growing because we have been taught to receive the power of God's Spirit, to listen to what he wants (*come and receive*) and he wants us to have an outward focus and be actively present in the local community because we genuinely care (*and overflow*).' At the time of going to press the church has moved into a fresh phase of strategic planning that both builds on the past and equips for the future.

5. They Are Able to Think and Act Incarnationally and to Give Themselves Sacrificially to the Task

It should come as no surprise that leaders of growing congregations are displaying mission-shaped leadership.

Readers of *Mission-Shaped Church* will have noticed that there is a close tie (but not an exact match) between the values of missionary churches and in particular the five marks of mission,[34] and these five leadership qualities equated with leaders of growing churches. I readily admit to being one of the many who have been deeply influenced by this seminal report. However, the overlap of values is not just a convenient construct. Those values were there and were legitimately observed during the research. It should come as no surprise that leaders of growing congregations are displaying mission-shaped leadership. The report has some challenging things to say about the role of leaders in fresh expressions of church. I want to suggest that there is a link between some of the shortfalls of leadership in fresh expressions of church and similar shortfalls in inherited patterns of church. There has been a tendency for fresh expressions to fail after the first generation leadership moves on. This indicates that leadership and ministry has been offered from one cultural setting to another, rather than embedding itself in the new culture. The report speaks of a need for leaders of fresh expressions to adopt a Christ-like strategy and 'die to' the culture of any sending or planting church so as to truly 'take root' in the new settings. Such arguments could well also be applied to inherited patterns of church. In the Anglican Church there is a history of inspired and gifted new incumbents bringing about something fresh in a parish for eight to ten years and for that to break down when they move on if it has not truly taken root in the broader leadership and the spiritual culture of the parish. The incumbents in my study were all aware how hard growth is to initiate and how easy it is for momentum to be lost. All were seeking through discipleship (another mark of the mission church) to get the vision and the values shared as widely as possible and were experiencing some success. The majority of them began to experience growth whilst relatively new in post, and worked in settings where the soil was prepared and people were ready for change. However, there was one notable exception to this which forms our next case study.

Case Study 7

Canon Keith Turner served two curacies in bustling suburban churches and moved from a Nottingham suburban church of 300 worshippers to take on a very different kind of role as Priest-in-Charge and subsequently Rector of the two villages of Papplewick and Linby, north of Nottingham. That was in 1983, and Keith and his family are still there 22 years later. The culture change was huge. These are real villages with the attendant pace of life and traditional resistance to change. Keith quickly became aware that he needed to be in there for the long haul. Over his early years the congregation learned to respect, to trust and to come to love the vicarage family. However, at the end of his first five years very little had actually changed. Step by step positive changes trickled in. A faith-sharing team from a local church were well received, an *Emmaus* group was started, links with local schools strengthened and an All Age Service was introduced. Fellowship deepened through away weekends and little by little growth occurred. As often happens questions began to be asked about how the physical structure of the buildings might be adapted to facilitate growth. Now, coming into their twenty-second year, Keith is leading the parish in a major building and fund-raising campaign. Numbers are still not vast. However,

At the end of his first five years very little had actually changed

the morale of the focus group was very high and there was a genuine sense of excitement about the future that is all too rare in rural parish settings. The history of the Church of England is full of stories of clergy who have stayed too long, having lost any vision or passion that they ever had. Keith's is the rare gift of the sustained envisioning of a leader sacrificially given to the task for the long term.

4 Making Use of This Booklet

Some Suggested Exercises
(These three pages may be photocopied)

From Chapter 1

1 Take Some Time to Review Your Experiences of Leadership

- What have you done over what period of time?
- What has worked well?
- What has not gone well?

If you have moved to a different leadership setting, to what extent are you just reliving what you have done before? Do you find yourself having another go at what did not go well in the hope that it will go better next time? Has the time come to face up to what you cannot do in order to concentrate on what you can do?

2 Has the Time Come for a Paradigm Shift in the Way You Do Leadership?
How would you know? Are there training opportunities run by your denominational leadership to help you address issues like this? Are you aware of colleagues asking similar questions and can you get together with them in a study group?

Look at the growth/decline chart (Figure 1). Remember this chart only describes statistics for the Diocese of Southwell, but the chances are that figures for your area will not differ that greatly. Absorb the truth that the difference between decline and growth may not be as great as you previously thought.

Absorb the truth that the difference between decline and growth may not be as great as you previously thought

Remember that tides come in as well as go out. Share this truth with other leaders you know and encourage one another. Ask what it means for the work you are currently involved in.

From Chapter 2

Are there churches near you that are experiencing moderate growth? Ask yourself if there are any obvious reasons why this is the case. Can you take a little time out to go and worship at these churches on your own or with others from your church? Is there a mission advisor for your denomination who can help facilitate this process? Are there opportunities to meet with the leader(s) of the growing church? In my experience most leaders of moderately growing churches are more than happy to meet with others. It is the leaders of mega-churches or well-publicized new expressions of church who can become overwhelmed with such requests. Remember that most leaders of moderately growing churches are pretty much like you — they both need to receive encouragement and like to give it.

> *Remind yourself that however you may feel today, your gifts have been recognized by others*

From Chapter 3

1 The Spiritual Gift of Leadership

If you are an ordained leader take out your licence to minister. If you have not already done so, have it framed and put it where you can see it every working day. Remind yourself that however you may feel today, your gifts have been recognized by others and you have been chosen for the job you are currently doing by others who were prayerfully seeking God's will on the matter! If you are a lay leader, remind yourself of the process by which you were selected. Take some time to be encouraged. God is at work in your work.

2 Think and Act Strategically

Focus on a project you are engaged on or about to begin, then apply these criteria:

- what is going to be done?
- by whom?
- with what resources?
- in what timescale?
- accountable to whom?
- monitored by whom?

Work at this with others in your leadership team. If you do not have such a team, co-opt someone!

3 Think and Act Relationally

Borrow David Rowe's five points from the Wilford strategic plan, asking what would be required to achieve these five aims in the church where you lead.

- Make church welcoming and user friendly
- Run events that encourage quality relationships
- Improve communication throughout the church family
- Build friendships in which we can tell our faith story
- Encourage wider participation using the whole variety of our gifts and talents.

This could be an exercise for a PCC or a parish away day.

4 Think and Act Transformationally—See Visions, Dream Dreams
This time borrow Peter Brierley's five headings and answer these (God) questions for your own setting.

- Where are you? (God to Adam; Genesis 3.9)
- What is in your hand? (God to Moses; Exodus 4.2)
- What are you doing here? (God to Elijah; 1 Kings 19.9)
- What do you see? (God to Jeremiah and Amos; Jeremiah 24.3 Amos 7.8)
- Can these bones live? (God to Ezekiel; Ezekiel 37.3)

5 Think and Act Incarnationally (and, if Need Be, Sacrificially)
Ponder the following reflections. Ignore them or respond to them as God directs.

- There is a time to ask, 'What is written in my contract?'
- There is a time to ask, 'What do I need and what does my family need?'
- There is a time to ask, 'Is this an appropriate career move?'
- There may even be a time to ask, 'Should I give up?'

But

There is also a time when the Spirit of God moves in the heart of a leader and when his answers blow away all of the above. At these times the question becomes: What would Jesus do? The answer to that might be that he would bleed and die that others can live!

He may say 'Give 22 years and more to that little country parish.'

He may say 'Stand in that cold church with 19 people and see 100 through the eyes of faith.'

That is the adventure of leadership!

A New Testament Perspective 5

Peter as a Leader (with reference to his response to the vision described in Acts 10)

To get the most out of what follows you will need to read Acts 10. This study may be photocopied for group use.

Peter was identified as one with the gift of leadership by Jesus himself. Jesus places on him a heavy burden: leadership of the very first 'expression of church.'

> 'And I tell you that you are Peter, and on this rock I will build my church.'
> (Matthew 16.18)

Some of us as leaders have struggled when replacing a notable predecessor, finding it hard to live with their ghost. How must it have felt for Peter to take over from Jesus? If ever there was a leader who led a church into growth it was Peter. The early chapters of Acts see the residual group of 120 followers of Christ quickly explode to a group of several thousand. Yet the scope for growth during that period had a very real limitation. Peter was a Jew and conceived of the good news as 'for the Jews.' Like Jesus, Peter saw the mission field as 'the lost sheep of the house of Israel' (Matthew 15.24). However, in response to growing persecution Peter found himself preaching further and further afield in an increasingly diverse context. In *Mission-Shaped Church* language, he was moving from the dechurched to the unchurched[35] (the lost sheep of the house of Israel to Gentile lost sheep). Was there a fresh expression of church for these people? The God-given answer came when the vision, which redefined clean and unclean, coincided with the arrival of a preaching opportunity among the Gentiles. In the context of this booklet we can learn from the way that Peter as a leader managed this new 'God-given' opportunity for growth and seek to apply the lesson to our 21st Century setting.

Peter not only heard God but was able to make the link between the vision and the opportunity. Leaders show the ability to think and act strategically, and when this is combined with the ability to listen to God they become the means by which godly change can happen. *Mission-Shaped Church* urges a process of double listening. We need to listen to our traditional understanding of God and we need to listen in the fresh context into which God has spoken. Peter acted quickly but not so quickly that he missed the opportunity to involve the church in this emerging new insight. As he made the journey from Joppa to the Gentile city of Caesarea, some of the Jewish brothers from Joppa went along. Whilst acting strategically Peter is also promoting strategic activity in others.

Peter thought and acted relationally in order to promote a good relationship between the Jewish church and this emerging Gentile church. Peter describes how his own understanding has changed: 'I now realize how true it is that God does not show favouritism but accepts those from every nation who fear him and do what is right' (Acts 10.34). He stresses his ordinary human status which makes the miracle that God works in ordinary Jews and ordinary Gentiles (and ordinary churches) all the greater. He carefully anchors what has happened, showing it to be the out-working of Jewish Scripture but clearly affecting Gentile seekers. By the end of the passage Jew and Gentile are celebrating together. Peter successfully led the church through a massive transition that opened up the gospel to millions more people.

Questions

1   What kind of vision does God set before leaders today? Has he been speaking to you?

2   What are the opportunities that accompany the vision in your area?

3   Are there people you should be taking with you on the journey?

4   How do we handle those who do not welcome or celebrate the change?

5   To what extent does honesty about our status and our ability to make mistakes make us vulnerable, and is this good or bad?

Notes

1   G K Chesterton, *The Everlasting Man* (San Francisco: Dodd, Mead and Company Ltd, 1925).

2   J Currin, *How to Develop a Mission Strategy* (Grove Evangelism booklet, Ev 68).

3   D Bosch, *Transforming Mission* (New York: Orbis, 1991).

4   MODEM is an acronym for Managerial and Organizational Disciplines for the Enhancement of Ministry. MODEM was set up in the mid 1990s with a vision statement: 'That by the year 2000 the values and disciplines of those engaged in the management of secular and Christian organizations will be mutually recognized and respected.' The organization runs a number of helpful seminars where those in ministry gain insights from those in secular management.

5   B Pettifer, 'Human resource management' in J Nelson (ed), *Management and Ministry* (Norwich: Canterbury Press (for MODEM), 1996) p 194.

6   S Bruce, *Religion in Modern Britain* (Oxford: Oxford University Press, 1995) p 37.

7   P Brierley, *The Tide is Running Out* (London: Christian Research, 2000) p 9.

8   D McGavran, *Understanding Church Growth* (Grand Rapids: Eerdmans, 1970) cover synopsis.

9   Brierley, *op cit*, p 9.

10 B Jackson, *Hope for the Church: Contemporary Strategies for Growth* (London: Church House Publishing, 2002) pp 37, 39.

11 G Cray (Chair), *Mission-Shaped Church: Church Planting and Fresh Expressions of Church in a Changing Context* (London: Church House Publishing, 2004).

12 M Booker and M Ireland, *Evangelism: Which Way Now? An Evaluation of Alpha, Emmaus, Cell Church and other contemporary strategies for Evangelism* (London: Church House Publishing, 2003).

13 R Warren, *The Healthy Churches Handbook: A Process for Revitalizing your Church* (London: Church House Publishing, 2004) p 84.

14 C A Schwarz, *Natural Church Development: Handbook* (Stirling: British Church Growth Association, 3rd edition, 1998).

15 For those unfamiliar with Anglican structures an Area Dean is a widely used alternative title to Rural Dean. The job of such Deans is to exercise a variety of leadership roles within clusters of parishes known as deaneries. The average size of a deanery is 12 parishes. Within the diocese of Southwell Area Deans

have an additional role in developing deanery strategies and overseeing apportioning of a share of the contribution to diocesan administration. Most Area Deans are also incumbents.

16 The Southwell diocese is divided into two Archdeaconries. The southern Archdeaconry is dominated by the Nottingham conurbation. The northern Archdeaconry is more rural with the largest individual towns being Newark, Mansfield and Worksop.

17 R Harden, 'Church sees an increase in its attendance' *Church Times,* 14 January 2005.

18 A T Le Peau, *Paths of Leadership* (London: Scripture Union, 1983), p 30.

19 J Lawrence, *Growing Leaders* (Oxford: Bible Reading Fellowship, 2004) p 57.

20 P Brierley, *Leadership Vision and Growing Churches* (Footscray: Christian Research, 2003) p 12.

21 B Hybels, *Courageous Leadership* (Grand Rapids: Zondervan, 2002).

22 J Lawrence, *Growing Leaders.*

23 J Lawrence, *Growing Leaders,* p 200.

24 R Pointer, *How Do Churches Grow?* (London: Marc Europe, 1984) pp 132, 167.

25 R Warren, *The Healthy Churches Handbook: A process for revitalizing your church* (London: Church House Publishing: 2004).

26 Jim Currin, Grove Evangelism booklet Ev 68 *How to Develop a Mission Strategy,* especially chapters 3-5 which cover in turn three steps of a mission and evangelism strategy—The Preparation, The Prayer and Planning Conference and The Follow Up.

27 R Warren, *The Healthy Churches Handbook,* p 106 figure 1.

28 W C Wright, *Relational Leadership* (London: Paternoster, 2000) p 2.

29 P Brierley, *op cit,* p 3. In her recent booklet in this series, Alison Gilchrist offers practical strategies for bringing about a change in culture (Grove Evangelism booklet, Ev 66 *Creating a Culture of Welcome in the Local Church*).

30 W C Wright, *op cit,* pp 116 and 117.

31 P Brierley, 'Get up and go!' in J Nelson (ed), *Management and Ministry* (Norwich: Canterbury Press (for MODEM), 1996) p 129.

32 P Brierley, 'Get up and go!', pp 130–9.

33 R Williams and M Tanner, *Developing Visionary Leadership* (Grove Renewal booklet, R 17).

34 G Cray (Chair), *Mission-Shaped Church,* p 81.

35 *ibid,* p 37.